The Wicked Teenager

The Savage Hangover

Archie's hands are trembling like humming birds

(See page 96 for text)

The Wicked Teenager

SOCIAL STEREOTYPES FROM THE
Telegraph magazine

Victoria Mather
and
Sue Macartney-Snape

JOHN MURRAY

First published in Great Britain in 2007 by John Murray (Publishers)
An Hachette Livre UK company

1

Text © 2006 and 2007 Daily Telegraph plc and Victoria Mather

Illustrations © 2006 and 2007 Daily Telegraph plc
and Sue Macartney-Snape

Foreword © 2007 Gyles Brandreth

A CIP catalogue record for this title is available from the British Library

ISBN 978-0-7195-9670-4

Typeset in Monotype Bembo 11.5/15pt by
Palimpsest Book Production Limited, Polmont, Stirlingshire

Printed and bound by L.E.G.O. SpA, Vicenza, Italy

John Murray policy is to use papers that are natural, renewable and recyclable products and
made from wood grown in sustainable forests. The logging and manufacturing processes are
expected to conform to the environmental regulations of the country of origin.

John Murray (Publishers)
338 Euston Road
London NW1 3BH

www.johnmurray.co.uk

Foreword

ESSENTIALLY I AM a town person. To say that I *loathe* the country-side would be an exaggeration, but only a slight one. I have a metropolitan soul. In any city – whether it is Manchester or Mumbai, Chicago or Cape Town – I feel at ease. In a capital city – such as London or Paris, or even Ottawa or Oslo – I feel properly at home. It is not just that I want to be where the action is (though I do – and how!); it is that, in every way (from a practical, aesthetic, even a spiritual standpoint), I prefer the urban to the rural. I prefer lamp posts to trees, pavements to pastures, the anonymity of the crowded corner coffee shop to the enforced bonhomie of the cosy country pub.

That said, I do go to the country. Many of my best friends live there. My wife likes to see them now and again, and expects me to come too. All of my enchanting godchildren (I have five or six: my wife knows their names) are country-dwellers, and to mark special moments in these young people's lives, their well-intentioned parents invite us for the weekend. When, briefly, I was a Member of Parliament, I found (to my horror) that a number of my constituents lived in villages and on farms. (I applied for the seat on the strength of its name. It was called 'The City of Chester'. It did not take me long to discover my mistake – nor my electors to discover theirs.)

I go to the country when I must and when I do, when I reach the land of chill winds and green wellies, I have only one consolation, one solace, one feature of the 'country weekend' that gets me through the ghastliness of it all. Invariably, in the guest room, on the bedside table, I will find a slim volume of 'Social Stereotypes' culled from the *Telegraph Magazine*.

I am happy to tell you that, over the past decade, there is not a single country house I have visited (be it a stately home or a converted barn) in which I have failed to find at least one book in this wonderful series. For a man marooned in the middle of nowhere, these small tomes are lifesavers. They bring the world to wherever you are and they anatomise that world with a brilliance, sharpness and wit that take your breath away.

It's so wretchedly quiet in the country that inevitably I wake up before dawn. But I don't mind, because at my bedside I know there will be a collection of 'Social Stereotypes' to divert me. It is indescribably dull in the country, but I don't care, because while the rest of the house party is out walking or stalking or twitching or driving over hill and dale to yet another pointless point-to-point, I am curled up with two amazing women. As a wise and wicked observer of the fashions, frailties and foibles of the age, Victoria Mather belongs to a rich English heritage that stretches from Geoffrey Chaucer to Evelyn Waugh. As an eagle-eyed illustrator, Sue Macartney-Snape belongs to a tradition that runs from William Hogarth to Ronald Searle.

This is their ninth collection of 'Social Stereotypes' – and their best. I have three children who have recently been teenagers. My offspring and their friends are to be found on every page of this remarkable little book – spotlighted, skewered, celebrated, kebabbed. I salute the genius of Mather and Macartney-Snape, the great illuminators of our age and the saving graces of the English country-house weekend.

Gyles Brandreth
London, 2007

For Rachel Wrey who was,
Leonora de Ferranti, Tilly Standing and Louis Levi who are,
and Sophie Coleridge who will be: wicked teenagers all.
Keep up the good work!
V.M.

For my niece Poppy who is my inspiration
when it comes to teenagers
S.M.-S.

THE MODERN TEENAGER is an awe-inspiring object to its baby-boomer parents. It can't spell or, like, speak. Duh. Yet it is technically fluent – every home should have one to sort out Sky Plus – infinitely better travelled and has titanic stamina. Think clubbing.

Thanks are again due to Michele Lavery, editor of the *Telegraph Magazine*, and Paul Davies, Denis Piggott and Jeremy Farr who tend the column weekly. I wrote most happily at the Mount Nelson Hotel, Cape Town, so thanks for the memories to Nick Seewar, the sleek general manager, and Pippa Isbell of Orient-Express. Many characters within have been inspired and illuminated by contributions from Mark Andreae, Christian de Ferranti, Daisy Finer, Tom Konig Oppenheimer, Santa Montefiore, Patty Palmer-Tomkinson, Vicki Reid, Sarah Standing, George Threlfall, inspiration for The Savage Hangover, and Rachel Wrey. At John Murray we thank Roland Philipps for creating the annual tradition of Stereotypes volumes, and Caroline Westmore has been saintly in her patience. In an era when publishing has become a hyper-market hell, nothing could be kinder or more personal than the care taken by Caro.

I recently heard a story proving teenage entrepreneurial subversion. The mother sweetly thought her daughter was taking chill bags of healthy fruit back to school: actually Persephone had injected oranges with vodka from her parents' drinks cupboard, frozen them and was selling the high-octane sorbets for a fiver each to the sixth formers. Wicked.

Victoria Mather
London, 2007

The parents don't, like, get, like, how really hard stuff is

The Wicked Teenager

POPPY HAS WORKED really hard all morning. She's downloaded lots of iTunes, and that was so tiring she, like, had to read about Brad and Angelina in *Hello!* Now Chloe has rung to say that business studies really sucks, and won't it be awesome when they get to Corfu, and did Poppy know that Tarquin is coming? Poppy says that's so cool, and wonders, as she varnishes her toenails, if she should have a little dolphin tattooed on her ankle. Mummy wouldn't really notice.

The Voice of Doom is currently calling up the stairs. 'Are you working, Poppy? I promised Mrs Hatchet that if you came home this weekend you would work six hours a day.' And Poppy shouts back, 'OK, Mum, yeah, like I'm doing some really good research on *As You Like It* on Google.'

This is guaranteed to fob off the parents, who are in despair about Poppy's English. 'Dad's really, like, annoying, Chloe, cos he keeps saying he did *As You Like It* at O level, you know, like, back in pre-history, and our spaniel could understand it. He doesn't, like, get, like, how really hard stuff is.'

Poppy's father is convinced his daughter's Shakespearean expertise consists of thinking Romeo is a Catapult who died on the *Titanic*. When Mummy said would Poppy like to go to the library and get some books 'so you can read round the subject, darling?' Poppy recoiled as if bitten by a puff adder. Books are so not cool, besides being, like, long. What she needs are, like, the answers to the questions. That's the way, like, to do exams. Her father fulminates about original thought, and Poppy says, 'Whatever, Dad' and fiddles with her LK Bennett shoes. Dad says Poppy understands less about the sonnets than a three-toed sloth. Poppy's vagued off: she's yearning for her hair straighteners and *Vogue*. She'll get an A.

9

The National Hunt Punter

DERMOT IS IN the equine heaven of Prestbury Park. He doesn't care about the vile wind whisking over the brow of Cleeve Hill, or the noise of helicopters bringing wealthier punters, like fighter craft over the Mekong Delta.

It is Cheltenham National Hunt Festival, and from the great roar before the Supreme Novices' Hurdle to the discarded betting stubs after the concluding County Hurdle, Dermot loves the smell of money in the morning. Is Racing Demon going to be the new Best Mate? What is the insider gossip on Kauto Star?

Over from Ireland, Dermot is staying with Eva and Bingo Lavishe in the Cotswolds. Their dinner parties are never less than 18 – 'Otherwise what is the point of having a cook, darling?' – the champagne and cigar intake is heroic and, after the rigours of bridge and backgammon, no one ever goes to bed before 2am. Dermot is thriving on this demanding regime.

The Lavishes have a box (it was dreadful once staying with the Meenes who failed to realise that the ideas 'March' and 'picnic' were incompatible) and a butler proffering electric soup. 'Would sir like a Bloody Bullshot?' And, sotto voce, 'Sir might like to consider State of Play.' Sir might well, and bungs the Jeeves a tenner.

From this nirvana of oysters and Filet of Beef Rossini – thank God there is nothing new-fashioned about Cheltenham – Dermot can slip into the mud-sodden concourse that is the gamblers' Glastonbury, into the melee of trainers, owners, Irish priests, bookmakers, duchesses and diminutive jockeys.

It is the only occasion when being small, cold and Irish is truly distinguished. When it is a privilege to be a sardine united in kinship with JP McManus, just another punter, albeit the grandest, in racing's crucible of gossip.

Cheltenham's the only occasion when being small, cold and Irish is truly distinguished

Krystal and Craig are united by an ability to hip-swivel

The Ballroom Dancers

KRYSTAL AND CRAIG are into their time steps: backwards, forwards, one-two-three. And smile. Krystal only hopes she hasn't got lipstick on her teeth. Although the samba at the Palais de Glide may not be *Strictly Come Dancing* – and Craig is certainly not Mark Ramprakash – Krystal has her pride. Her hair is lacquered into a profiterole pyramid, her fake tan is so subtly pale as to imply verisimilitude, her armpits have been waxed.

Craig has, of course, had his chest waxed and his chiffon silk shirt and hip-hugging black trousers have been sourced from dancepants.com. He is going to Cuba for his hols to try out the real thing. Krystal – and smile – wants to slap him every time he says. 'Thread your leg between mine, luv,' and prompts a clutch-twirl with an ingratiating grimace of his ferrety molars.

Krystal and Craig don't really know each other, they have been united, as on a blind date, by an ability to hip-swivel, and hatred is their energiser. She suspects he is a graduate of flamenco classes at the Tush'n'Tequila in Bexhill-on-Sea. Craig thinks Krystal is a piece of work, particularly when they go past the compère and he calls out, 'Well, Krystal, may I say that you are looking exceptionally lovely tonight?' Craig's getting a stiff neck and a sore back for this? To be Billy Zane to her Claire Bloom? The cha-cha-cha is one thing, but to be ig-ig nored is quite another.

Krystal – and smile – meanwhile has sequin-cramp on her left breast from Craig clutching her to him during the tango. However weird it is struggling with the shimmy, the jive and the paso doble (the waltz is for wimps), Krystal knows she is consuming 250 calories per half hour of twist-grind murder with Craig; he is inspired by his teacher, Colin, who says, 'Dance is an essential centre for well-being.' And smile.

The City Bonus

RICK DID NOT betray by a myopic blink or a trembling hand what he thought of his bonus. The pre-Christmas ritual was as ever; envelopes on the boss's desk, and the one marked with his name slipped across with ameliorative remarks about a fantastic year and 'Your splendid contribution, Rick. Sadly, there were other departments that let the side down, so this is not as much as I would like to be giving you.'

The boss isn't receiving a bonus of his own of £30 million for lack of perspicacity: he can detect a tiny vein throbbing involuntarily at the corner of Rick's eye, magnified by the Gucci specs.

He knew, as did the interested crowd beyond the glass walls of the CEO's brutally modern office, that visions of Rolex watches, holidays in the Maldives, perhaps a Lamborghini Murciélago, were ticking behind Rick's forehead like the Bloomberg Index.

Meanwhile Rick said neutrally, 'That's fine, and I'll talk to my team,' and exited pursued by relief that he didn't just get £200,000 – which is for bottom-feeders and those being told in no uncertain terms to look for another job – and horribly thrilled that he is now going to put his guys through the same ritual humiliation with their bonus details.

Other people's Januarys are so dreary; but Rick's is full of buying a loft apartment pre-wired with a Bang & Olufsen sound system and putting his black credit card behind the bar at Umbaba so all the mates and chicks can enjoy fabulous amounts of his fizzy friend, Jerry Boam. He's bought PJ time in Net Jet, so he doesn't have to rub shoulders with the football strip people at airports, and chartered a yacht in Croatia for the summer. 'Is Robbie Williams going to perform at your 30th birthday party?' the mates tease. Rick isn't telling. That's his speciality at Deutsche Gromit.

*Rick has visions of Rolex watches, holidays in the Maldives,
perhaps a Lamborghini Murciélago*

Lady Sproat, dressed for a wedding, has a comforting talk with the terrier man

The Boxing Day Meet

LADY SPROAT HAS descended upon the Fur and Feathers both as a Gesture of Support and a way of giving her verminous relations something to do with their livers. Over breakfast (kedgeree deep-frozen in October and barely thawed in an Aga exhausted by its exertions with the turkey), she announced that everyone was to be on parade at 10.30am. 'Including you, Gideon. The Master needs us.'

Hermione Sproat considers Gideon to be an unsatisfactory son-in-law (why couldn't Lettice have chosen a decently impoverished landowner?) and uses upon him the gimlet eye that has reduced several lefty vicars to pulp. Dressed in assorted coats and welling-tons from the boot room, the house party and the dogs pile into the Land Rovers – dogs in the front, grandchildren in the boot – and then into the bar. Gideon is setting up Bloody Marys, Lettice is on her second cup of mulled wine, three of the dogs have picked fights with sofa-dwelling Pekingese mistakenly brought out for a treat, and one grandchild's been reversed into by a horse's bottom.

Lady Sproat, dressed as for a wedding and drinking port, has sailed through crowds sporting Christmas jumpers to have a comforting talk with the terrier man, who is also her plumber. Around them swirl tweed-jacketed children on Thelwell ponies and chaps in new hunting kit, vulgar were it not for the fact that they've taken up the sport in the cause of civil liberties.

The Master, who remembers Lady Sproat's days riding side-saddle with the Herriard, doffs his cap. Then he stands in his stirrups and shouts, 'We will be hunting within the law, following a trail, and doing hound exercise in the afternoon.' PC Sloley, who's been conversing companionably while eating mince pies, nods complicitly. Satisfied, Lady Sproat musters her troops back to Sproat Hall for cold ham and baked potatoes.

17

The Compost Enthusiasts

CONSTANCE AND CAROLINE have long since abandoned their nephew's wedding reception. They disapprove of the modern wedding, which seems to them to last a great deal longer than the modern marriage, but Ned has undoubtedly married well. His in-laws' compost heap, discovered during a snoop around the garden, is a thing of joy and beauty that would not shame Lady Eve Balfour, founder of the Soil Association.

Constance considers the carbon-to-nitrogen ratio excellent: too often the Dave-come-lately composter overdoes the browns (dried flowers and cardboard, God help us), lacks fresh grass cuttings and fails to chop the greens (asparagus, old bits of cabbage). Caroline feels an overwhelming urge to plunge her hands into the dark soil and inhale the sweet, earthy smell, better than Arpège.

This is the epitome of the soil-plant-animal-plant-soil cycle, the essence of wholeness and nature. Constance and Caroline absolve their dear new niece Cressida's parents – whom they'd regarded with huge suspicion for living in Hertfordshire, a non-county – from succumbing to Smartsoil, the composting revolution from Sweden. Mature compost in four weeks is not Lady Eve. Six months to two years is the poetry of decomposition they are now contemplating. Caroline can see a lovely, happy worm. The only site to which she has subscribed on the internet is the Worm Man (international delivery). Constance saw slugs on Cressida's mother's lettuces: 'Too marvellous, there can't be a smidgeon of insecticide.'

Recalled to the wedding dinner, she tells the young man on her right how young nettles are an excellent compost accelerator. Caroline talks to the PR director on her left about how Cleopatra declared the earthworm sacred. 'They are an ecotoxicological sentinel species, you know.' Everyone thinks they're marvellously New Tory.

They plunge their hands into the dark soil and inhale the sweet, earthy smell, better than Arpège

In the nether world of back martyrs, each has their own guru

The Back Sufferer

ROGER SAYS IT'S an old sporting injury, implying a glorious rugby career in the First XV. Roger says 'Oh dear, it's my back' a lot, particularly when asked to take out the rubbish. There's much clutching of the small of the back and swaying while grimacing apologetically as his wife Sue, heaving suitcases down the stairs, mutters under her breath that perhaps if Roger lost his paunch his bloody vertebrae might not be so stressed.

Any journey or trip to the theatre is preceded by the ritual of Hunt the Back Cushion. Aeroplanes require a doctor's note requesting an upgrade due to intense suffering. Then there's the Tens machine, a black box worn on Roger's belt which sends electric currents to the affected lower back. Supposed to be soothing, it afflicts Roger with a unique form of prickly heat. He can tell you all about it, ditto the impossibility of sleeping without a pillow between his knees to relieve the pain, as recommended by his back doctor. 'Marvellous chap, any back problems, I can give you his name.'

In the netherworld of back martyrs, each has their own guru, osteopath, healing hands naturopath, Alexander technique wizard, New Zealand physiotherapist ('She's superb, you mustn't see anyone else') and can spend happy hours discussing having their spines cracked by chiropractors. Then there are the epidurals for drastic relief When It All Gets Too Much. Roger can impart more awesome detail than a woman who's had several epidural births.

When he does his spine curls on the sitting-room carpet, getting in everyone's way, Sue thinks there are decidedly three people in their marriage – him, her and the back: 'What about Pilates to strengthen the wretched thing?' Everyone has learnt that the one thing you never, ever ask Roger is, 'How are you?'

The Bikini Buyer

LOLLY HAS LEFT it too late. The shops are now full of thick tweed and Christmas decorations, oblivious to her need for a chic September holiday in Paxos. 'The sea will really have warmed up over the summer.'

But Lolly is not going to be able to get into this balmy blue briny because the only bikinis left in the universe are on the sale rail, size eight. In orangey-yellow. Not a good look with bottom-crêpe and orange-peel thighs. Pin-thin friends smugly advised Lolly to go to Heidi Klein, where it's summer all year round, but Lolly wanted the motherly environs of a department store, not a couture disco where two bits of material tied together with string cost £150. Even more horrible than cruel changing-room lighting is the inverse proportion between the amount of material deployed in a bikini and its price tag.

When did her bottom become the size of Wales? She's been sitting on it for so long she never noticed. Lolly wants to die of shame, and that's before the deforestation humiliation of a bikini wax.

Now, in the lonely raw fluorescence of Women's Fashions, Lolly sees before her, blobbing in the mirror, a great big pear with her head mysteriously stuck on the top. Why oh why is it her bottom that has blossomed, not her bosom, which has obstinately retained pimple status? One size does not fit all in bikinis; Lolly obviously needs a bandage for her top and a bin bag for her bottom. Apparently Elizabeth Hurley designs separate tops and bottoms, but it's all very well for her, isn't it? She's size nothing.

Bitterness is setting in. Lolly's vision of skipping in the Ionian Sea is fast receding. Why didn't she opt for a holiday at the North Pole where she could have dressed like a duvet? On balance, Lolly thinks there is a great deal to be said for a burqa.

When did her bottom become the size of Wales?

Art fails to pierce the miasma of teenage apathy

The Cultural Outing

GODFATHER MARCUS HAS taken Harry to the National Gallery. The trip's been talked up all week by Harry's mother, Sasha: 'You are a lucky boy, Marcus is taking the day off from Christoby's. Isn't he kind?' and 'Many people would give their eye teeth to be going to see the Renaissance pictures with a world expert. I'm thrilled to be tagging along.' Yet her desperate enthusiasm has failed to pierce the miasma of teenage apathy. Sasha catches Harry texting in front of a Raphael Madonna and makes frantic don't-you-dare movements, while trying to look rapt as Marcus explains Raphael's visual achievement of the Neoplatonic ideal of human grandeur.

Duh. Whatever. Harry thinks Madonnas are dumb. Isn't Madonna some old slapper in suspenders who sings cheesy music? Multi-faith studies at Harry's school having sidelined Christianity as non-PC, he is fatally indifferent to Baby Jesuses, Crucifixions and Assumptions. 'I'm sure you can see the clarity of form and ease of composition, Harry. Vasari said Raphael's paintings are living things.' Marcus is appealing to Harry's hidden depths. Harry is equally adept at keeping them hidden. When Marcus attempts popular culture with a reference to *The Da Vinci Code*, Harry says, 'That was a really dumb film', and is pinched hard by his mother as Marcus laughs good-naturedly. The glaucoma of boredom vaguely clears from Harry's eyes at the description of Leonardo as anatomist, working on dead bodies in his studio. 'They must have seriously ponged.'

The only other flicker of interest he emits is in how much the pictures are worth. 'They're priceless, Harry. Their incomparable value is their beauty which pierces the human soul.' Harry looks weaselly. 'You're always selling pictures by these dudes at Christoby's and they get millions.' Marcus says tightly that he's glad his godson reads the arts pages. All end up feeling distinctly brittle.

25

The Old Little Girl

MITZI ONLY LOOKS normal during the festive season, dressed, as she is year-round, like a cross between the fairy on the top of the Christmas tree and Raine Spencer.

Age has withered her and the years condemned, something of which she is sublimely unaware since her fashion clock stopped when her Papa told her she looked pretty in pink. An only child, she has no siblings to inform her of the brutal truth that bows are unfortunate after the age of 12.

Mitzi's progress through parties is a fragrant reminder of Christmas past. She speaks of champers and nibbles, and how Papa always had an oyster bar at their Christmas parties in Eaton Square, with the oysters being opened by a sweet man from Scott's. She leaves a whiff of lavender in her wake.

At grand private views Mitzi is sometimes accompanied by a relic of Ruritanian royalty, the Duke of Montenegro or a Serene Highness with Hapsburg connections. Afterwards she will take them to dinner at the Ritz – the charming pink dining room abundant with cherubim offsets her froth of silk tulle perfectly – and sign the bill.

The advantage of being an heiress is the complete insulation from real life. Very little unpleasant has ever touched Mitzi, other than her mother bringing her out in countless seasons and shrieking at her for not attracting young men. Mitzi and Papa thought young men callow and vulgar. 'I couldn't lose you to one of those whey-faced chappies, could I, poppet?' said Papa.

In a funny old way she's very happy as an eccentric gargoyle lionised for her colourful appearances in society, and tottering down Elizabeth Street during the day, with the poodle, to buy novels at Henry Stokes and have a nice chat about engraved stationery. It would've been nice to be a duchess, but perhaps too tiring.

Bows are unfortunate after the age of 12

*Nipper and his snarling colleagues at Zoom Delivery
are cultural icons*

The Cycle Courier

NIPPER CONSIDERS HIMSELF to be an urban anti-hero, a lithe leopard in Lycra, although everyone else thinks he's a menace. Particularly the infirm, tottering along the pavement on a brave little expedition to get the *Evening Standard*, and Latvian au pairs wheeling pushchairs to the park while talking on their mobiles. Nipper weaves in between them, a stealthy streak of speed like a bullet grazing their cheeks. By the time the infirm have wheezed 'Keep to the road, young man' and the au pair has checked that her ear, her mobile and her boyfriend on the other end of it are all still in communication, Nipper is through the red light.

Like a swallow in summer, Nipper is now seasonal king of the road. Motorcycle couriers are fat bastards. Nipper and his snarling colleagues at Zoom Delivery are cultural icons and have inspired international designers with their street style: it says so on wikipedia.com – Nipper's mate Skip forwarded it to Nipper's Treo while he was waiting for a job at Canary Wharf. Waiting's not so bad in a good summer. Nipper'll have a latte and an energy bar, and take his skid-lid off and run Gore-tex hands through gel-slick hair.

He presents a frightening sight, like a skinny red, orange and black beetle. He's also the curse of post rooms, since instead of carrying his cargo in a pouch in front, like a bicycling kangaroo, Nipper opts for the macho, aerodynamic option of a load double-strapped on his back, necessitating a sweaty striptease flailing tattooed arms.

Then he'll be away on his fixed-gear bike, thumping on the gridlocked cars of drivers at Blackfriars who give him the finger for hogging Queen Victoria Street. A good thump makes his day, leaving the imprisoned driver apoplectic at the sight of Nipper's taut bottom pedalling away.

*A conversation punctuated by the whistling of
Reggie's hearing aid*

The Deaf Guest

REGGIE HAS JUST turned to Foxy Pettigrew, saying, 'Sorry, m'dear, you've got my bad ear, where did you say you were from?' and Foxy is shouting, 'I'm staying at Marchmont, with Peregrine and Pooh.' It's the curse of the country dinner party – she's always next to someone deafened by shooting. From the moment Reggie cupped his hand round his good ear what-whating at her, Foxy knew she was in for a conversation punctuated by the whistling of Reggie's hearing aid.

Over the smoked trout terrine Reggie barks questions about who Foxy's people are, which chap she is married to and (rather too loud) 'You mean that red-faced cove at the end of the table? Got a drink problem, I shouldn't wonder,' while helping himself to another glass of Pomerol. The ear-cupping means Reggie's turned his back on the woman on his right and Balmoral rules of switching conversational partners between courses die with the pheasant à la Normande. Foxy's got him until the cheese, after which she profoundly hopes her hostess will step back into the 19th century and remove the ladies to the loo, leaving the men to the port.

Reggie, meanwhile, is in high gig. This Roxy seems a jolly sort, if a bit gummy. At least with a big mouth like that he can see what she's saying. He thinks they're having rather a good chinwag about South Africa; he talks about the Boer War battlefields, she talks about her safari. The aural amalgamation of Spion Kop/safari whistles through the deaf ear and Reggie thinks they are as one in their own soliloquies. Foxy's jaw aches from articulating slowly.

Later, turbo-charged by a cigar, Reggie lumbers into the drawing room seeking 'my Roxy fascinator'. Foxy has left, pleading a sore throat.

When did their little darling transmogrify into this volcano of stuff in bin bags?

Back to University

WILLOW HAS BEEN saying, 'OK, yah, Mum, like, I'll really help in a minute, but I must text Emily cos we're going to Max's rave tomorrow night, see?' Mum does not see, nor does Dad, who fails to understand why his daughter appears to have no suitcases, only bin bags, and has spent the last hour languidly eating cereal and toast, mobile clamped to her ear, while her long-suffering parents have toiled out to the car with the contents of her wardrobe. Nor does he consider the collected works of Jilly Cooper to be the intellectual cornerstone of a course in anthropology.

'Honestly, Catherine, how did you manage to bring up your daughter without the ability to read? Did she just choose anthropology because it began with A? I suppose we must count ourselves lucky Newcastle University wasn't offering a course in aardvarks.' Catherine mutters through three togs of duck-down duvet that Willow is Geoffrey's daughter too.

The car is heaving with pillows, laptop, iPod docking station 'Whoah, Dad, be careful, will ya?' – knives, forks, plates, sugar, pasta, Weetabix, Marmite and kettle which Willow won't use, 'Cos why else did God invent Starbucks?' Catherine comforts herself with this minute indication of Willow's interest in theology.

When did their little darling transmogrify into this volcano of stuff, as Willow calls it. 'Oh, it's just my stuff, Dad' is now being fought into the Toyota Prius, and the dog has to sit on the duvet between the avocado plant and Teddy.

At the other end the stuff has to be shoehorned into a prison cell with a steel basin. The farewell is interrupted by Willow's calls from Ben and Ed and Josh. At the last moment, she rushes up and hugs her old fossils in their embarrassing car. 'Mum, Dad, you've been amazing. I love you lots. And don't worry – I've got Jilly and Teddy.'

The Pet Funeral

THE DEMISE OF Gretel the guinea pig is being treated with due solemnity in the Armitage family. Luckily Florence didn't hear Daddy saying thank God the bloody thing had snuffed it. 'I had to wrench up the floorboards every time it escaped from its cage; that Gretel was the Houdini of the guinea pig world.' But Daddy has done what daddies have to do in the circumstances: dug a poignant little grave under the apple tree. Mummy has sacrificed her best designer shoebox as a coffin, as Gretel was not a Russell & Bromley sort of guinea pig. Gretel was an Agouti, her hair speckled with gold, silver and cinnamon. Gretel ate sweet clover and canteloupe melons. She is being interned on a bed of hay, with a Cox's Orange Pippin for her journey to guinea pig heaven.

There has been much discussion about readings for Gretel's funeral. Daddy favours adapting Martin Luther. 'I always thought the chap was a dead bore until I found out he believed dogs have souls. Now, Florence, how about "Be comforted, little guinea pig, thou too in the Resurrection shall have a tail of gold"? Probably the very thing Gretel would like after a lifetime with a sawn-off bottom.' Floods from Florence. Mummy hugs the bereaved. 'There, there, darling, when we lose a friend they become a new star in the sky. Gretel will be twinkling down on you.' Florence's brother Jake points his fingers down his throat in sick-making motions. He's always teased Florence mercilessly about guinea pig being the national dish of Peru, yet he didn't relish being the one who found Gretel claws-up in her cage. So Jake makes the wooden cross, Mummy picks spring flowers from the garden for the funeral wreath and Daddy delivers a eulogy to a 'furry little butterball and chewer of cardboard'. Then they have consolatory crumpets for tea.

*Gretel the guinea pig is being interned in Mummy's
best designer shoebox*

The Cleaner

OLGA COMES FROM a small East European country of which her employer has never heard. So he calls her Olga-from-the-Volga and she calls him Meester Paul and dusts him to death. The flat, drenched in filth under the aegis of Mrs Moppit, who had rheumatics and a fatal attraction to the drinks cupboard, is now sparkly. Olga clatters over the wooden floor in enticing shoes, carrying her bucket bristling with lemon Cif, Pledge wipes for blond wood, Mr Muscle for blasting the bath and nuclear bleach for the lavatory. Olga does not hold with limescale in any form and is constantly poking at plugholes with severe wire brushes and viscous descalent.

Paul, who works from home, is unable to have any little word with Olga about breakages (frequent) because she perpetually conducts machine-gunfire conversations into her mobile in Easto Europeano. It is so alarmingly guttural that when Aunt Maud's vase crashes to the floor its demise can hardly be heard. Paul feels humbled in the face of what are obviously Olga's complicated domestic arrangements, organising her relatives coming over to England and advising them about benefits. She clearly has a much more demanding social life than he does and, frankly, at least he knows his fast disappearing objects are safely broken, not stolen.

Olga can also iron, a talent that eluded Mrs Moppit. Indeed, Olga can iron and talk on the mobile and listen to the radio all at the same time. She can also cook very brown, hearty food since, unlike either his mother or Mrs Moppit, she worries about him. 'Meester Paul, you do not eat. I make you goulash.' It is marvellously like school food. If paid the requisite £10.50 an hour, Olga will do dinner. His friends are entranced by her smile and the parts of her fore and aft bursting out of the apron. Crashing the few remaining plates into the dishwasher is her speciality.

Olga perpetually conducts machine-gunfire conversations into her mobile in Easto Europeano

The 4x4 Victim

ARTHUR HAD NOTHING to do with the purchase of this hate-mobile. Honestly. He and Teddy are weally, weally embawwassed by it. Arthur's school run has not been the same since Mummy insisted on driving the 300 metres to his Church of England primary in her new Sioux Obstwuctor.

Perfectly nice people shake their fists at Arthur and Teddy in their steel and glass cage. Mummy can't see over the dashboard, so the zebwa cwossing is irrelevant to her progress down the narrow street. Pedestrians scatter beneath her wheels; au pairs wrest pushchairs from bull bars more suited to Helmand province.

Arthur is particularly struck by pensioners tottering on Zimmer frames caught in the Obstwuctor's downdraught. He's rapidly learning how to lipread invective. 'Mummy, that man said you were a rich witch. Are you, Mummy?' When Mummy said she was going to have her hair coloured, Arthur wanted to know if it was a special colour called You Bloody Blonde.

Arthur's friend Cosmo, whose mother takes him to school on the back of her bicycle, says Arthur is ruining the planet and it's all because of him and his stupid car that there soon won't be any more polar bears. 'Mummy, what are carbon e-missiles?' 'Something Daddy sends from the office, darling. Eat up your broccoli.'

On his way to Mandarin Chinese classes Arthur is marooned at every traffic light amid a sea of furious, grimacing faces. He and Teddy are isolated in their moving entertainment centre, with their DVDs and Comfy-Wumfy car seat, while outside the world turns to look at them with righteous loathing. Particularly the woman who's splashed as Mummy drives through a puddle.

'Mummy, what does plucking tewwowist mean?' Mummy can't hear. She's on her phone.

*Arthur and Teddy are weally, weally embawwassed
by this hatemobile*

Chantal's red-carpet etiquette is more ruthless than anything devised at the Court of the Sun King

The Clipboard Nazi

CHANTAL'S MISSION IS to make sure that nobody she considers a nobody will get into the party being given by a Russian oligarch at the Serpentine Gallery in aid of Ukrainian orphans. The minor celebrity from *Hollyoaks*, arriving with eleven best friends in search of free caviar and vodka, doesn't stand a chance.

This is when Chantal deploys her earpiece, which is not actually connected, seemingly negotiating with the powers that be within. She can drag this out for as long as it takes for the loathsomely wrong guest to be humiliated in front of the paparazzi and decide to go to Boujis.

Chantal was not brought up in a Manchester tenement without acquiring impressive life skills. She will both recognise and be oleaginously nice to Kylie's stylist, has the psychic powers to detect Orlando Bloom behind his curtain of hair, and is as warmly welcoming to the actress wearing Armani as she's chill to the weather girl wearing Next. 'How are you spelling Tracey? I'm afraid I can't see your name on the list. Anywhere.' Chantal's work at Glitz Communications consists of not communicating with the riff-raff, while gushing over the useful, the Next Big Things and the scandal sensation du jour. Out with Paris Hilton, in with Alastair Campbell. Gives the other guests something to talk about. Colleen is the babe of the year, although Chantal hopes she doesn't bring little potato-face. Chantal doesn't do ugly, or people who owe her money, or anyone she overhears calling her a door whore.

Her red-carpet etiquette is more ruthless than anything devised at the Court of the Sun King. On former prisoners, Jonathan Aitken is acceptable, Lord Archer most definitely not. GlitzCo prides itself on such fine distinctions and Chantal can deliver a 'Have you got your invitation, sir?' with the poisonous charm of a cobra.

The Easter Egg Hunt

SAM HAS SNAFFLED most of the Easter eggs because he took the precaution of waking early to kneel at his bedroom window watching Mummy and Daddy hide the boodle. Sam is thus smug. Polly is tearful. She stupidly relied on fair play.

Daddy is limping because he had to climb the oak tree to hide Mummy's bird's nests full of speckly sugar eggs. 'Honestly, Amelia, don't you think the children are too old for all this? I know I am.' And so he dramatically fell the last metre, possibly snapping a ligament in his knee. He really thinks he has; in fact, he can feel the swelling.

Mummy, who's been up since 5am making the bird's nests out of raffia, has terminal exhaustion and is not in the mood for a Man to Be Ill. 'However, if our luck holds, Edward, and Sam and Casper from next door beat each other to death with chocolate rabbits, I can take a job lot of you to hospital.'

Polly is still crying, molten sobs hiccupingly punctuated with 'It's not fair'. Polly is a wuss, so she couldn't climb the tree to get the pretty, speckly eggs. 'It's not fair.' Casper's sister Lucy is a tomboy and she got two nests – 'It's not fair' – but her mother is furious about the bark-green stains on Lucy's new Jigsaw skirt. This is fairer.

Amelia is now telling Edward (in the hissing whisper of furious marrieds) that he's bloody lucky he isn't being made to be the Easter Bunny, as he was when Sam and Polly were really little. 'And why don't you bloody get some champagne on the go?'

Way before the paschal lamb, Sam is going to be demented on E-numbers. Polly will hoard her eggs in her bedroom and, annoyingly, not eat them all at once. Casper and Lucy say the speckly, pretty eggs are disgusting. They'd prefer Celebrations. It's not fair.

Sam is smug, having cheated; Polly stupidly relied on fair play

Mylene's Romanian, guttural imprecations are an instrument in her armoury of intimidations

The Fitness Torturer

MYLENE IS THE personal training equivalent of Rosa Klebb. Spartan in spandex, a muscled, toned reproach to flab and cellulite. Mylene is mean. No New Year's resolution to be a better, fitter person is going to flag under her watch. Men are terrified of her evangelism about core strength. All flail like flatfish on the mats, feeling fat bits of themselves squidging around their elasticated waistbands and wondering whether it will ever be possible, in this lifetime, to emulate Mylene's washboard stomach. Mylene says yes. Or rather 'Yerrrsss', for she is Romanian and her guttural imprecations are another instrument in her armoury of intimidation. 'You do the 20 sit-ups now. Now. Now. No resting. Why eez you groaning?'

She shames her clients into running the extra mile on the machine – 'Faster, faster. That eez walking' – until they feel their bones are crumbling to dust and their hearts popping out of their mouths. No one argues the toss with Mylene, they're too breathless. Men strongly suspect that Mylene can crack walnuts between her thighs.

Does she eat broken glass for breakfast? 'No, I eat pulses. No wheat. The wheat it bloats the stomach. Why eat it if it 'ates you?' So that's toast over. Any attempt to get chummy with Mylene founders on her draconian discipline. 'Come and have coffee with us, Mylene?' 'No, coffee eez a stimulant.' She also disapproves of sparkling water – 'Eet puts air in zee guts' – and herb tea in teabags. 'You must make eet fresh.' It's not difficult to imagine Mylene in her flat, brewing up healthy concoctions smelling of silage.

Yet after a month the gasping and wobbly are a bit fitter and firmer; some have glimpsed a muscle. In Mylene-speak, they have tiny breakthroughs of feeling grrrreat. Who would have thought her savagery would result in being love-bombed by endorphins?

The Emergency Pee

CECELIA IS IN extremis. The Crawford-Cromptons have given a lavish party in their Fulham garden, but thrown all their money at the marquee and champagne and cheese-pared on Portaloos.

The tent was so crowded with bushy-eyebrowed men trumpeting 'Wah-wah-wah, eh?' across the canapés that Cecelia couldn't get to the loo in the house. Dinner became a cross-legged agony. Now Monty is standing *cave* by a merciful bush outside the local park.

'Righty-ho, no one coming, old girl, quick sharp. Appalling things go on in public parks these days, worse than public lavatories. You could have waited until we got back to the Sloane Club. I feel a chump holding your handbag.' Cecelia hisses that he doesn't know how lucky he is being a man, for whom watering the rosebed is a traditional activity accompanied by a cigar.

Monty harrumphs that the most consistent tradition in their marriage has been him staking out Cecelia's puddle stops. 'You were incontinent when we married at 25. Don't you remember that layby near Pitlochry where I had to hold up a groundsheet?'

Cecelia protests that only Monty would have considered that a camping holiday in the Highlands was a suitable honeymoon. 'Well, think of the times we've had to go to Claridge's because you think every other ladies' in the West End is beneath you. So to speak.'

Cecelia says Claridge's has Floris, and a nice lady filling the hand basin and giving one linen towels. 'If I'm in Chelsea, I always go to Peter Jones.'

Monty is puzzled as to what this has to do with anything, other than a kindly gesture of Cecelia's towards egalitarianism. She certainly doesn't do motorway service stations; theirs will forever be a marriage measured out in detours off the M4 to find Cecelia a suitable hedge.

*Cecelia was cross-legged in agony; Monty is standing cave
by a merciful bush outside the local park*

The Last Smoker

ORLANDO IS LATE, wafting through the door breathing Krug and
Marlboro. Miranda is so prostrate with relief that her only spare man
has actually turned up that when Orlando says, 'Do you mind awfully
if I smoke?' she hasn't the heart to send him out into the garden.
'Oh no, please do,' she says feebly. 'Now, let's just find an ashtray.'
There follows a lengthy scrabbling in cupboards, punctuated with
the apologetic 'I know we've got one somewhere', and 'Do you
mind using a coffee saucer?' and the lighting of Diptyque candles (I
couldn't borrow your lighter, could I, Orlando darling?) to mask the
ciggie smell with Feu du Bois. 'So lovely, smells of old churches.'

In the consequent fug, the non-smokers who swear they've given
up smoking, but have actually just given up buying cigarettes, sidle
up to Orlando with a hearty 'Delighted to see you're being so
politically incorrect, mate. Mind if I bum one?' Will Cadger says
he really gave up after his last duty-free trip to Lille on Eurostar
when his first-class ticket and lunch at a Michelin-starred restau-
rant 'cost me £180 to save £140 on something that was going to
kill me. Ha, ha. Could I just sneak the one?'

Sukie, seated next to Orlando at dinner, has decided that he's so
gorgeous that she's going to take up smoking. His smutty eyes look
as if they've been put in with ashy thumbprints; his floppy hair is
what's meant by ash-blond. Sukie's overdone the white wine.

Miranda's dinner party has been overturned by boys from behind
the bikesheds. Her slow-roasted shoulder of lamb with 23 cloves
of garlic is suffocated by nicotine: Orlando smokes between courses
– 'Darling Randa, you are such heaven not to mind' – and no one
eats anything. Next day they all ring and say what fun it was meeting
Orlando. Miranda's house, repeatedly fumigated with jasmine room
spray, smells of ashtray for a week.

Orlando smokes between courses and no one eats anything

Going Dutch

DILLIE CHALLONER MET Priscilla Crosby in the market in Charmont-sur-Ciel. After a morning dealing with the bloody French (the plumber is at the end of his 35-hour week and won't come and unblock the loo – quelle pongo), she was thrilled to see a Notting Hill neighbour. There was a lot of 'Darling!' from Dillie, and astonishment from Priscilla. On home turf Dillie normally reverses over her in a 4x4 with rear vision obscured by shopping bags.

Now united on foreign soil (Priscilla was outraged that the Toulouse-Lautrec museum closed for lunch), they agreed to meet at Chez Jacques.

The husbands actually get on rather well (Tristram Crosby makes documentaries, Alex Challoner is in commercial property) until the bill arrives. Priscilla doesn't drink and only ordered an omelette and a green salad. Tristram had the *plat du jour* and no pudding. Dillie and Alex had everything. The kir royales were flowing by the time Priscilla and Tristram arrived. 'We're two up, go on, spoil youselves. Come on, Prissy, have a kir Perrier. Live a little.'

The Challoners order foie gras, then Dillie has lobster and Alex has chateaubriand, with béarnaise and chips. He orders a Pouilly Fuissé and a grand cru Bordeaux. Then another with the cheese. 'Yo, Tristram, leave the Rwandan genocide, or whatever your last docu was, on one side – have a brandy.'

When the bill comes, Alex says airily. 'Let's just split it down the middle.' But when Priscilla says, 'But I didn't drink and I only had an omelette,' the Challoners look at her as if she's committed social suicide. There's achingly slow negotiation betwixt cash and credit cards, and how much to leave as a tip. 'Trick of sharing the bill, darling, is always order the most expensive thing – spreads it around a bit,' Alex says, as he pockets the receipt for expenses.

'Let's just split it down the middle'

*Giles's Riva says what a phenomenal proportion
of the £858 billion in hedge he personally made*

The Hedge Funder

GILES HAS ALL the kit: house within the congestion zone, Euro-wife with collagen implants, a Lexus with bull bars for the Croatian nanny to take little Saskia to kindergarten. And a Riva. It's the ultimate speedboat, his St Tropez toy that says he is probably responsible for a phenomenal proportion of the £858 billion swishing about in hedge funds globally.

He can certainly talk the talk about pension funds, endowment funds and corporate money, in between ordering the crudités and rosé at Club 55. His wife vagues off (it's so difficult getting raw cauliflower through her plumpy lips) as Giles sounds off about equity markets soaring, institutional money and 'You may have read what I said in *EuroHedge*.' She is thinking clubbing at Les Caves du Roy.

It's the beginning of the season; Giles can set the benchmark for buying the most expensive bottle of champagne. He gave the most expensive children's party for Saskia: all the three-year-olds had their own butlers with white gloves. There was Laurent-Perrier pink champagne for the mothers, 'which contributed hugely to the 20 per cent increase in pink fizz sales in the UK,' says Giles, with his careless aptitude for confusing a joke with a statistic.

He's now got a really serious problem. The airstrip at the Greek island he's rented for the summer is two feet too short for the private jet he's chartered, so this requires another island for the plane to land on, plus a yacht to be chartered to get the house party to the original island. But hey, *Hedge Fund Intelligence* says there's an 8.8 per cent jump in investment and Giles is in the clover up to his Prada sunglasses. What's a little island between friends? Just as long as no one has a bigger and better Riva.

The Hallowe'en Hostess

MARY-LOU JUST wanted, for one night only, to turn Phillimore Gardens into Greenwich, Connecticut: neighbourly (if an American gated community is your idea of neighbourly), a friendly mom-and-apple-pie scene of carved pumpkins and incy-wincy spiders. Her role as an American banker's wife will be fulfilled by networking along the white porticoed doors of the street, trick-or-treating the film producer with the home cinema, the Oscar-nominated composer and the countess whose paint is peeling. Particularly the countess. 'Say, we have children the same age, would your gang like to come play with Connor and Piper?'

Mary-Lou booked the caterers for her Hallowe'en party in July; there are sandwiches in the shapes of bats, cats and rats. Also green jelly served on black lacquer trays and very orange muffins made of pumpkin. The cocktail sausages are skewered on miniature broomsticks. Poppet Events has festooned Mary-Lou's garden with orange lanterns, orange fairy lights and iridescent ghosts suspended in the trees. They're sound-sensitive, so the slightest movement makes them go woo-woo, which interrupts all the American banker dads' calls to New York on their BlackBerrys.

Mary-Lou has hired a face painter to turn Piper into a Very Nice Rat, and Connor has told everyone at Thomas's School about his Superman costume.

Bowls on the hall table abound with slime gobstoppers and chocolate beetles, treats when the doorbell rings. Ding-dong. Duane and Wayne are strictly not Greenwich, CT, where feral youth has been sanitised. 'So give us a treat, Mrs.' Mary-Lou says would they like to sing a song for their chocolate beetle? 'No, Mrs, we'd like cash.'

Mary-Lou sees their pimples glinting orangely in her fairy lights and knows she'll never get this English hug-a-hoodie thing.

Mary-Lou doesn't get the English hug-a-hoodie thing

Re-entering fatherhood in the Harry Potter era,
Bunter is at the sharp end of parenting

The Older Father

BUNTER DOESN'T HAVE quite the same allure as Michael Douglas when he takes young Ptolemy to playgroup. He doubts that Rod Stewart changes nappies, although Paul McCartney probably did, which is strangely creepy.

There is a fine line between being a hip modern father and a sad dad. Tolly loves bouncing around on his father's tum, but it makes Bunter's back ache dreadfully. Still, what a jolly soul the little chap is.

Bunter doesn't remember much about the babyhood of his first brood, now in their thirties. He was always working late at the office and his former wife dealt with the nursery, only presenting Susan and Richard to their father after he'd had a stiff whisky. They would obediently listen to Beatrix Potter as a treat.

Re-entering fatherhood in the Harry Potter era, Bunter is at the sharp end of bathtime, lowering himself like a camel to kneel on the bathroom floor. He was always frightened of drowning Susan and Richard; now he's got more confidence and is capable of handling Tolly and a rubber duck at the same time. Of course he got a ribbing when Jessica became pregnant; and there was tut-tutting from her mother about how he'd be too old for the fathers' race.

Several chums at the Reform Club remarked that it was obvious he still had plenty of snap in his celery but they didn't envy him the sleepless nights. He is, indeed, exhausted. 'But it's in a good way, isn't it, darling?' Jessica says as she leaves to work on a three-day film shoot in Manchester. 'So, it's you and me, young man. Let's crack open the Cow & Gate and I'm going to read you some Keats.' Bunter has no intention of embarrassing his son by playing football with him, but he's damned well going to make sure he knows the classics.

Oenone drank the water of the Ganges when she went to an ashram at Rishikesh

The Indiaphile

OENONE IS MEDITATING in Shimla. Every Indiaphile knows that it is too hot to be on the plains at this time of year, but to be in the Himalayas (which Oenone calls the Him-MA-lee-ahs) is perfection. So she's having aromatherapy at Wildflower Hall, being basted in the spa with healing oils, and her reflex points titillated to promote physical and mental wellbeing.

Oenone's Damascene conversion to India came on the trip to Rajasthan for Rolly Prendergast's 50th birthday, the one and only time Mr Oenone braved Delhi belly and poverty – 'Not my bag, but Rolly's a good chap, was with him at Oxford' – and she Found Herself in a charming temple. She won't talk about it specifically, leaving her spiritual enlightenment wrapped in Marabar Caves mystery. 'But I only eat pulses now, and hardly drink alcohol, just Himalayan water.' This is tricky in Shropshire.

That first journey was one of forts and palaces and maharajahs with whom Rolly was at Eton; he and their chums clung to Imodium and Kingfisher beer, while Oenone wandered into the village, had chotas made in every colour, and was undismayed when Rolly asked her whether she thought she should be wearing pyjama gear at her age. Now she goes alone, with a tapestry bag full of Smints, wetwipes, lipsalve, Paul Scott's *Staying On*, her passport in a Ziploc bag, a spare pashmina in case of savage air conditioning, her digital camera and Nurofen Plus. She is never ill and drank the water of the Ganges when she went to an ashram at Rishikesh.

She's going to have a rice and buttermilk treatment to exfoliate her skin before returning to Delhi and the soothing environs of the Imperial Hotel, with its engravings of elephants confronting tigers, and native insurgents. Back in Shropshire the fading henna on her hands will look like a communicable disease.

The Post Office Queue

WHY CAN'T ONE go to the post office and just buy a stamp any longer? Or do anything simple and have a little chat with the postmistress, who's now from Gujarat and sitting behind an iron grille?

Steam is coming out of Mrs Scimitar's cast-iron perm because all she wants to do is collect her pension. She has staggered to the top of the queue ('M'legs aren't what they were, love') and is now stuck behind a man transferring money to Montenegro – just when she thought that by wheezing, and rootling at their ankles with her walking stick, she'd bypassed the Polish builder with the red T-shirt (sending money to Krakow) and the arty type with his poncy purple scarf (buying travel insurance to go to Thailand and do druggy things on beaches, she shouldn't wonder).

She is cross. The Pole is cross, so is the artist, also the blue-rinsed Mrs Slocombe lookalike, and the furry-eyebrowed old colonel who's having to get his European Health Insurance Card because his daughter-in-law says otherwise she won't be responsible when he comes to stay in the house in France. In fact, volcanic crossness has gripped everyone in the eternal queue.

There is council tax to be paid and the exchange of saving stamps for car tax, and the Jamaican lady in green wants to switch to Post Office HomePhone.

People's feet are killing them, and small children voraciously express acute hunger pangs. They may die of starvation – directly beneath the poster saying one can make donations here for the latest famine in Ethiopia – in the time it takes to explain the Post Office's new policy on payment per envelope size. Everyone in the queue covertly thinks that everyone else – with the possible exception of the old colonel – is claiming illegal benefits.

It's lunchtime and only two counters are manned

Shannon is basically living on Trill

The Health Faddist

SHANNON IS FRAUGHT with anxiety. She knows that Himalayan goji berries contain more iron than spinach, 500 times more vitamin C than oranges and are a richer source of beta carotene than carrots, but will they fight for ascendancy over her system with the acai berry juice from Brazil that's pulsing with antioxidants and polyphenols? Both contain pomegranate juice, but maybe the western pomegranates, star of Ipanema juice bars, will fight with the eastern, yogic pomegranates. The pomegranate's role as free radical scavenger and zapper of bad cholesterol may be lost in Pommy Wars, as 21 trace minerals and 18 essential amino acids slog it out in hand-to-hand combat in her bloodstream.

Shannon has espoused ginkgo to halt incipient mental fuzziness, omega-3 fish oils, plus milk thistle for her liver in case, in between anti inflammatory blueberry juice and antioxidant raspberry juice, she is tempted to try a glass of organic red wine to boost her heart. Breakfast is a feast of pills, augmented by seeds from the Food Doctor. Shannon is basically living on Trill.

Her yogurt is so live it greets her break-dancing in the fridge. Her chicken is so organic it comes with its name attached and a farmyard history attesting to its happy life. Fish is a terrible anxiety. Obviously it is good for one, but is one depleting fish stocks? Cod is clearly the eco-health faddist's nemesis. The chips are as nothing to the political consequences of eating cod. In her nightmares, caused by the indigestible consequences of mixed nuts, Shannon dreams of the North Sea as a polluted, empty void. She wakes with her heart beating and has to make green tea. The next anxiety is whether she should wear only organic clothing recognised by the Sustainable Texture Certification system. But most anxious-making of all is why Shannon always has a cold.

Milo's so emaciated by the drink and drugs during his days as a drummer that he's Chablys's perfect rockfest-cred

The Rock Festival Goers

CHABLYS IS AT the V Festival with her weird uncle Milo. He's so emaciated by the drink and drugs during his days as a drummer that he's her perfect rockfest-cred; a sort of tame Rolling Stone. Chablys, who's with the Whirlwind model agency, is desperate to be discovered in Kate Moss mode, negotiating the mud (an essential rock festival accessory) drainpipe legs exaggerated in wellies. The pout and the heavy lidded stare scream babe.

She painted her yurt herself, although Milo put it up for her in the campsite at Weston Park; 68,000 people all being cool is really stressy. Milo is staying nearby with posh friends in a stately. 'Doll, when you've been in rehab, camping is one too far. They're cool dudes, we grooved in the sixties, and you'll be able to come over and have a bath.' Thus, after one sleepless night sharing the yurt with her friend Jasmine, Chablys decamps to the Jacobite Bedroom. Forget the hey-man, joss-stick fug fantasy of rock festivals, with topnotes of marijuana, and the damp reality that stinks of burger stalls and beer fumes. She's much happier talking about Radiohead in the panelled drawing room; the earl knows David Bowie and the countess wears vintage Celia Birtwell. It's a scene. It has hot water.

Chablys and Milo therefore waft around the festival designer-dishevelled, as if artlessly tent-fresh, but they are actually clean. The flash of Chablys's iPod, her permanently lit cig and Milo's punky jewellery are all outward signs of inward disgrace: desperate camouflage for being establishment hippies. They can talk the talk about Paul Weller having headlined the first V in 1996 and have VIP passes to hang out with grungy old rock stars backstage, but come early evening they walk the walk – or rather zoom the zoom in the earl's Ferrari – towards some Krug. God, one has to have a civilised dinner before returning to dance to Faithless.

The Insomniac

DAPHNE HAS HIT the witching hour. It is nearly 3.30am; should she take a sleeping pill? Any later and she will be groping through bright, confident morning in a daze of Temazepam hangover.

Earlier, she had hopes that the BBC World Service would lull her to sleep, and indeed did doze fitfully during a report on the nutmeg harvest in Grenada. Normally the words 'Iraq' and 'Hamas' have an instantly somnolent effect (on a par with 'Northern Ireland' a decade ago), ditto the shipping forecast, but Daphne's nocturnal anxiety is such that she feels, in these troubled times, that the price of liberty is her eternal vigilance.

Daphne, having made herself a cup of herb tea and rubbed valerian essence on to her pulse points, is now reading by torch-light so as not to disturb Gerald, who is pushing up the zeds despite saying he never gets a wink because she is so restless. Hence the paraphernalia of torch and headphones, for Gerald is infuriatingly princess-and-the-pea-like about his kip. There's a lot of 'Couldn't you be quieter when you turn over?' and 'You're not going to read are you? You know I can't sleep with the light on.' Thus at the age of 50 Daphne has regressed to the school torch-under-the-bedclothes routine. Soothing re-runs of *The Vicar of Dibley* are out, even if the telly is shrouded with a bath towel; the flickering penetrates Gerald's retinas. Even if he is asleep. Daphne longs for him to go away on business so she can enjoy her misery in peace.

What she likes is to go to bed with Jeremy Paxman. *Newsnight* often precipitates a blissful two hours of oblivion before she first surfaces, heart racing and slightly sweaty, at 1.30am. After essaying two Kalm homeopathic pills she then makes lists: 'Remember to take Tiffin to the Vet' and 'Clean the Oven'. One advantage of being so exhausted the next day is that these tiresome imperatives are forgotten.

Daphne had hopes that the BBC World Service
would lull her to sleep

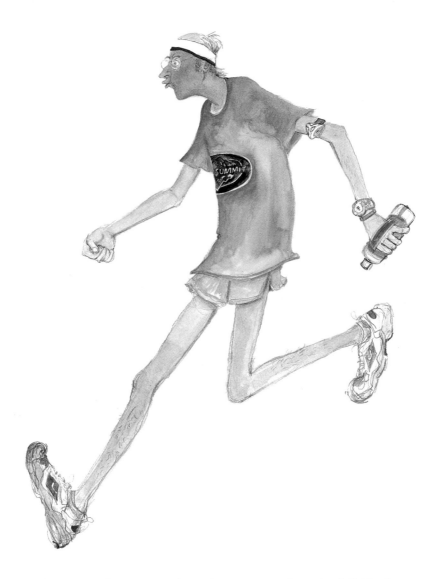

Seamus is fantasising about the moment when the foil blanket is wrapped around him

The Marathon Runner

SEAMUS HAS ANKLE instability, weak muscles up the insides of his shins, and his big toes don't bend as they should. As a marathon runner, none of this is good.

Seamus is an optician from Biggin Hill, and has entered the marathon for charity, although mercifully not dressed as Elvis. His sister has breast cancer, and Seamus is running to raise money for the Haven Trust, which has given her support and kindness. He drew the line at being dressed entirely in pink (Haven's signature colour), but he's going to finish the London marathon if it kills him. Which it has done to surprisingly few people in its 25 years – eight, according to St John Ambulance, which from 600,000 entries makes it less dangerous than snooker. Seamus likes this statistic. He is not the merchant banker sort of runner, who's stocked up on carbs at Cipriani's and runs while texting.

Seamus has been training since October, running on Saturdays around the park (with the dog, who's exhausted), a pedometer on his arm. He would like to complete the 26-odd miles in under five hours. Already he is fantasising about the moment when the foil blanket is wrapped around him and his dehydration and cramp worries are behind him. He has lost a stone in training.

He has forsaken alcohol, Diet Coke, Starbucks and crisps. His wife, Aileen, has learnt to make risotto (carbohydrate), baked potatoes with protein fillings and, while grumbling that she never wanted to open a Spud-U-Like, is dead proud of Seamus. 'He's not just a jogger, you know. He's doing the London marathon. For charity. Now, here's the form, pledge him some money.'

Seamus won't let anyone down. He'll never have been so tired, or so triumphant, and Aileen will give him a T-shirt bearing the legend, 'Never again – until the next time.'

The Maternity Nurse

ELAINE IS THE still, calm centre of the storm that has descended on the house since Baby arrived. Mummy is exhausted by demand feeding; the dog is so appalled by the squalling maggot in a cot that it's reverted to widdling on the doormat; Daddy's spent his sleepless nights cursing Dave Cameron's subversive example of hands-on fatherhood.

Then came Elaine, all spick and span from the Little Darlings Nanny Service. The baby instantly knew it was in the hands of a professional and stopped grizzling. Elaine gently but firmly put a stop to demand feeding. Routine, routine, routine is Elaine's mantra, and there must be no eye contact with Baby (wildly overstimulating) when Baby is put down to sleep. Mummy says weakly, 'Elaine, I can't handle controlled crying' – which is quite all right, as Elaine is there to handle it for her.

Elaine says Mummy should have Cotton Bottoms, an eco-nappy service for proper towelling squares. Does Mummy know how bad disposables are for the environment? Mummy is too fraught to care, what with recovering from the Gowri Motha gentle birth method, not eating wheat in case her uterus gets blocked by toxins, and agonising about whether she has bought the Bugaboo pram in the right colour. Elaine says Mummy should have reflexology and yoga at the Me and My Baby Clinic. Elaine's pronouncements, such as 'breast is best', are always accompanied by her hands being held in a yogic circle of energy.

Cooking Elaine's lunch, making her fresh mint tea and fulfilling her shopping list at the Organic Pharmacy are as nothing compared to the peace of mind Mummy and the dog now have about Baby.

Daddy is looking down the thick end of £1,000 a week; Mummy wants Elaine to stay for ever.

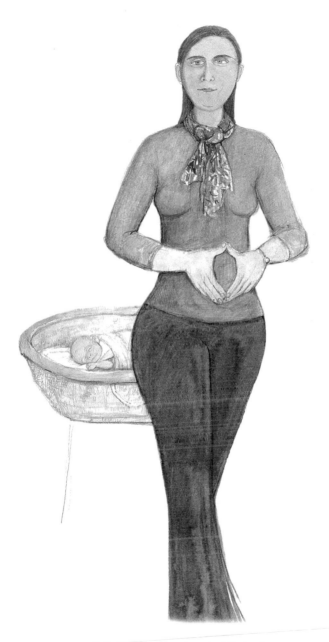

Routine, routine, routine is Elaine's mantra

*In the cacophony of explosions Hugo fails to hear
his small son wailing*

The Scary Bonfire Party

HUGO IS LOVING every whizz and bang. He counts along to the rockets backfiring in successive Technicolor rings. 'One, two, three, four, five . . . I say, darling, that was a fiver. Completely brilliant. Isn't this fun? The Piggotts' firework party is always the best.' In the cacophony of explosions Hugo fails to hear his small son wailing in his lonely eyrie on Dad's shoulders.

The idea that any red-blooded toddler wouldn't be entranced by an orgy of pop-pop, bang-bang is entirely alien. The Piggotts' annual party has been talked up for weeks. 'It's going to be such fun, darling, Porker Piggott works on it with a professional firework designer. Not even bloody 'Elf and Safety can defeat Porker. No damp squibs for him!' Little Finn has thus been expecting a humungous treat, together with sausages and ice cream, but has found himself in a bad night in Basra.

Mummy, swathed in shocking-pink fun fur, has overdone the mulled wine so is oblivious to her youngest's distress in the face of shooting stars and fountains of fluorescence. Muffy Sowerby (who has to be asked by Porker because she's a neighbour and otherwise 'Sour-will-be, ha-ha!') is eyeing them aghast.

Hugo reminisces about how Porker's firework parties all began when they shared a cottage at Oxford. 'Terrific girl pullers. There was a moment when a Roman candle went AWOL and sparkled up Candida Tiddly-Plunket's Afghan coat from Oxfam.'

The fireworks finale is an orgy of sound and light, during which Finn beats his father's bald head like a drum, which Hugo mistakes for ecstatic pleasure. The sizzling silhouette of the guy on the bonfire may be a happy vision of Osama Bin Liner to Hugo, but it will haunt Finn's dreams.

The Office Flirt

VICKI'S A CAUTION, she really is. Mr Grimthorpe (accounts) finds her ample bottom mesmerising, although he knows he shouldn't because with just one look he could be guilty of sexual harassment, and Mrs Grimthorpe would suffer the humiliation of reading about him as a filthy fiend in the *Evening Argus*.

Vicki means nothing by it, it's just a tease to brighten the long winter days at Weary & Dreary, purveyors of office supplies.

The only exciting thing that's happened at Weary & Dreary, apart from when Vicki's bottom wiggles like tectonic plates, is the explosion in the requirement for shredders activated by the scary stories in the *Daily Mail* about identity theft. As Vicki says to   Rupert in sales (with a confidential lean of her embonpoint), is shredding the new sex?

Rupert says, 'Get orff it, Vix, and I'll stand you a G and T at the Malibu Bar by the Vue cinema.' Vicki says. 'Well, you're a demon. Rupey, but it'll be just the one as I don't want our Shaun the husband thinking I'm hanging out with the riff-raff.'

Naturally, Vicki is the one in charge of the office party, although Mr Pillock (human resources) says absolutely not to her idea of inflated bosom balloons with hot-pink furry nipple rings. 'Now, Victoria, when I assigned you this role it was so that you could develop as a mature person. I was thinking mulled wine and mince pies, not sex toys. A Father Christmas hat for Mr Dreary is the most excitement I'll allow. Please do not disappoint me.'

Vicki is blissfully the last bastion of office subversion, and has sourced hazelnuts that, when cracked, reveal condoms in all colours. Eat your heart out, Mr Pillock. Together with the crackers full of frilly undies, Vicki has done Weary & Dreary proud, she knows about fun but it's all shopfront, innit, no follow-through; she's a good girl.

Vicki is blissfully the last bastion of office subversion

Phyllis and Naomi worship at the throne of the Donmar

The Theatre Friends

PHYLLIS AND NAOMI always go to the theatre together. Phyllis is recently widowed and Naomi's husband says he's not going to spend the evening being spat over by some woofter pretending to be Don Juan. Where is Brian Rix when you need him? Naomi says, 'Yes dear, your dinner's in the fridge. Cold ham,' and catches the 137 bus from Clapham.

She and Phyllis are Friends of the Royal Court and the Almeida; they like a theatre with a nice cafe so they can have a little supper before the performance, otherwise it gets too late for the bus home.

They worship at the shrine of the Donmar and are on the priority mailing list for the National Theatre, avid for the £10 tickets during the Travelex season. At the West End theatres Phyllis and Naomi cannily book seats with restricted view – often only £6 – then peer around their pillar just before curtain-up to see if the front row is empty, whereupon they beetle forward. This gives them both stiff necks, and the spittle danger is omnipresent, but it's as nothing to Being Part of It All. They've witnessed the beaded sweat of Michael Gambon and the wiglines of Maggie Smith. Crunched together at the Royal Court on a Monday (another £10 wheeze), they've seen the new Terry Johnson; fringe holds no fears for them as Phyllis's granddaughter acts with the Bread and Marmite Theatre Company so they go to performances in pubs. Being surrounded by old men with ponytails and girls in kaftans makes them feel excitingly inside-track.

Phyllis and Naomi will venture outside the metropolis, given a fair wind by a Charles Spencer review, to satiate their theatrical curiosity. Saver returns took them to the Theatre Royal, Bath, to check if the passage of time had diminished *Look Back in Anger* – 'A Peter Hall production, Phyllis' – to merely *Look Back in Slightly Cross*.

*Cheryl has the do-we-look-like-terrorists question
from fifty people a day*

The Check-In Girl

CHERYL HAS SEEN it all before. The husband furious with his wife for being overweight (not her body, but her suitcases), the wife being furious with her husband about the upgrade: 'What do you mean we're in row 30? I thought you'd spoken to Lord Plummit – does this woman know who we are?'

Cheryl has worked at Plummit Airlines long enough to know that she is going to be asked to look for a message in the computer: 'My husband is one of Lord P's closest friends. Lord Plummit would be very angry if he knew we were sitting in the lavatories.' Cheryl does a lot of spirited tippy-tappy-typing, but is actually messaging Jade at check-in desk 13 saying, 'There's a fat git and his Cruella wife in front of me – have you got a crying baby I can put them next to?' She emerges from this exercise smiling beatifically, Jade having found 18-month-old twins on the flight to Australia, and says, 'Madam, I'm afraid you are only allowed one piece of hand luggage, either your handbag or your overnight bag.' Cruella goes into a tailspin. 'You mean I cannot take my Hermès Birkin bag and my overnight case with my cashmere pyjamas? Impossible.'

Cheryl (who recognises a Bangkok market fake Birkin when she sees one) is now purring with the added insults of no lipgloss or liquids. 'What do you mean, girl? Am I to be deprived of moisturiser on a 23-hour flight? Can you just explain how I am going to blow up the plane with my Clinique glosstick? I tell you, my husband will speak to Lord Plummit. Martin! Get on your mobile, we cannot be treated like this. Do we look like terrorists?'

Cheryl has the do-we-look-like-terrorists question from fifty people a day. She calmly says, 'Did you pack your case yourself?' and 'Here are your boarding cards, sir, madam. Row 45. Have a nice flight.'

The Topiary Lovers

TOBY IS CONVINCED that within the 25ft lump of yew a peacock is screaming to get out. Tony is more of a cone and spire man. When they bought Millamant Court years ago, they were both in arts administration, dreamt of restoring the formal gardens, and read of the costume ball at Versailles when Madame de Pompadour, dressed as the huntress Diana, embarked on her career as a royal mistress by dropping her handkerchief in front of Louis XV dressed as a clipped yew. The romance of it.

Toby envisaged a topiary opera of cypresses, as described by Pliny the Elder in the first century AD, but in the end they went to lovely Harriet Sykes at Bellamont Topiary in dear Long Bredy, and bought balls of hardy Dorset box, and spirals of yew, like verdant Cornettos, to begin with. Harriet, successor to their idol Herbert Cutbush, the original British topiary nursery specialist, enthused them about cloud topiary, organic shapes like giant bonsai, but Toby's inner vulgarian suddenly burst forth. He did not need yogic green-growing feather pillows; he yearned for peacocks, for lions, for unicorns. He has seen Marylyn Abbott's Alice in Wonderland knot garden in Hampshire. Now, armed with a pair of shears, he's going to release a veritable ark.

Tony says, 'Calm down, dear, it's only a hedge,' but is exceptionally protective of his sculptural shapes which give formality to the garden. His bobbles of sweet bay, nurtured with crushed mussel shells, delineate the walk up to the south side of the Court. Neither Toby nor Tony would dream of emulating the American topiary artist Jeff Brees, who uses wire frames. A shocking cop-out for those gifted with the free hand and sharp secateurs. Toby hopes future generations will come to see his duck and seven ducklings intersecting the kitchen garden.

*Toby yearns for peacocks, for lions, for unicorns, but Tony
is protective of his sculptural shapes*

Henry and Virginia are terrified Svetlana is pricing their heirlooms for predatory marriage purposes to their son

The Unsuitable Girlfriend

SVETLANA IS AN exotic bird of paradise in the Old Rectory. Hampshire doesn't really do Russians, particularly those with platinum hair and no discernible underwear. Henry and Virginia are terrified she is pricing their heirlooms for predatory marriage purposes to their son. Charlie is bewitched, although one might have thought that a reassuringly dull young man working for Knight Frank would have been more a Sophie than a Svetlana chap.

He met Sveta when showing her a duplex riverside loft apartment costing a fraction of her bonus from Credit Suisse First Boston. Sadly she didn't like the taps – 'Gold is 'orrible'; not an opinion that applies to her jewellery – so she and Charlie had a series of assignations in ever more expensive properties with chrome fittings.

This is the first weekend with his parents, who kindly said that they'd not be changing for dinner on Saturday (after all, the poor girl's a foreigner and might not understand black tie) so are stunned that evening gloves are Sveta's idea of casual. Virginia notes that Sveta doesn't help to load the dishwasher, gets up at midday, has no wellingtons and makes Charlie run round her like a spaniel.

Also, Sveta fearlessly smokes. Henry has sworn that he's given up, but Sveta wordlessly slips him Marlboro Lights on the terrace. 'Just going to show Sveta the garden, Virginia,' he shouts heartily, scuttling off for a puff under the wisteria. Virginia thinks Sveta's interest in gardening is unlikely to be on a par with Vita Sackville-West's, but has to admit she's fearsomely clever. Far too well-educated (Sveta's read, and knows, Salman Rushdie) for Charlie, who went to Stowe. After she's left in her Porsche, like an alien departing in a spaceship, Henry and Virginia talk her up. 'Charlie is going out with a very stylish Russian girl, frightfully bright and cosmopolitan. We think she's a real breath of fresh air.'

Leslie and Rosemary are sashaying through Egypt,
living off fatted calves

The Tireless SKI-ers

LESLIE IS DETERMINED to Spend the Kids' Inheritance. His children are furious, foreseeing that whatever Gordon Brown's scam as Chancellor hasn't raided from Leslie's pension schemes is going to disappear into the hands of Messrs Abercrombie & Kent. Their mother, Rosemary, makes ameliorative noises: 'Darlings, it's time for us to have a gap year. Dad's worked so hard, and I can't really be expected to be a granny nanny service.' Leslie is cheerfully blunt: 'Given you a jolly good education and the starter payment on a flat. And you all got a car. Now earn your own money, like I did, and stop hanging around waiting for us to die.'

Even now Leslie and Rosemary (panting behind) are sashaying through Egypt, living off fatted calves. Leslie is an indefatigable tourist. Every mummy in the Cairo Museum has been minutely examined, every dusty fossil, when all Rosemary wanted to see was Tutankhamun's gold hunting dogs. She's now wilting in 30-degree heat at Giza while Leslie spouts stuff about the pyramids having been built to connect to the sun god Ra, creator of life.

Dripping, Rosemary doesn't care and is appalled by the fact that the Sphinx's sadly worn away nose is virtually touching a Kentucky Fried Chicken. Something Leslie's guidebooks do not reveal. She wants, with every bone threatened with arthritis in her body, to return to the air-conditioned nirvana of the Four Seasons, her novel, the pool and the spa. Leslie is game on for a Nile river dinner with a belly dancer show. He's also mugging up on all the Rameses for the Valley of the Kings while Rosemary fantasises about the Agatha Christie ambience at the Old Cataract Hotel.

Next up is their trip to Cambodia and Angkor Wat. Leslie has told the children that with Gordon's inheritance tax, 'It's kinder we don't leave you anything.'

The Anklebiter

MAUDIE IS THE scourge of postmen, meter readers and Jehovah's Witnesses. Mrs Gorringe adores her. While Maudie is capable of hurling herself at the letter box, ripping unpleasant brown envelopes from Postie's fingers, Mrs Gorringe has no need of a security system. She's safe from junk mail, since Maudie has a vociferous appetite for pizza flyers and sounds to the deliverers as if she's a pit bull capable of tearing them limb from limb. It is a pity about the window cleaner, who has refused to come to No. 9 Thatcher Avenue ever since Maudie imbedded her fangs in his ankle with the speed and venom of a black mamba. The plumber won't attend to the most catastrophic burst pipe 'Until your doggie is under lock and key, Mrs Gorringe', muttering 'Little bleeder' under his breath and donning industrial-strength boots. Mrs Gorringe, who possesses nothing as cruel and unnatural as a cage for her little bundle of joy, says 'Come into the garden, Maudie' and refuses to make tea for poltroons posing as handymen.

Men, indeed. She and Maudie are united in their dislike of men. Trousers are to Maudie as red rags to bulls. Mrs Gorringe was infinitely relieved when Mr Gorringe departed this life, leaving her in peace to watch the racing on afternoon telly. The puppy Maudie was given to her as a consolatory companion by the Gorringe son, Nigel, whom Maudie bit in transit. She stoutly resisted house-training; why on earth would one want to go outside when there's nice warm carpet? Nor does Maudie see the point of baskets when Mrs Gorringe has such a comfy bed.

The Gorringe grandchildren are now unable to visit lest Maudie savages them. Since Mrs Gorringe and Maudie are also united in their dislike of children, they live in perfect harmony.

Mrs Gorringe and Maudie are united in their dislike of men

The bits of Sven not poured into tight rubber are tanned and muscular

The Divemaster

SVEN IS THE new sex god. He is the underwater version of the safari guide and the ski instructor, the new best friend of the adventure traveller. Particularly the women.

Many are honeymooners who've been told they really must have something to do on honeymoon, so it's a PADI course in the Seychelles. After the first day with the fearsomely fit Sven, Pandora's eyes shining when he shows her how to spit into her mask to stop condensation, James realises he is an inadequate citified cypher. The bits of Sven not poured into tight rubber are tanned and muscular; James has white bandy legs that look acceptable only when poured into Anderson & Sheppard. Sven enters the deep blue sea sleek as a seal; James, when united with mask and flippers, looks like Dustin Hoffman in *The Graduate*. Sven knows the names of 57 different species of clown fish; the only time James has ever seen anything similar is in the fish tank in his dentist's waiting room. Sven helps Pandora, honey-coloured with Fake Bake, into her wetsuit; James is left flailing on the deck.

In the exotic underwater world, the divemaster is the source of all knowledge, his silent language of the thumbs-up and the finger circle meant to encourage and reassure. He is the omnipotent being between Pandora and Jaws.

Later, in the bar, showing James and Pandora his tropical fish books, the Big Eye Black Bar Soldierfish sounds thrilling in his Swedish accent. 'James, Sven has swum with sea lions in the Galapagos'; 'Sven has dived in the Shark Hole in Tikehau – it's in French Polynesia, silly – we must go. Wow! Pelagic fish are so cool.'

After spending thousands on a palm-fringed honeymoon, James didn't expect his wife's honeymoon souvenir to be the divemaster's e-mail address.

The Unhappy Campers

CELIA AND FRANCES are dismayed. They're unable to detect the cool camping phenomenon through the Cornish sea fret. Where is Sienna Miller in leopardette wellies when you need her? There is a Cath Kidston-ish floral tent beside them, but a man in a ginger beard crawled out of it; and he wasn't ginger in a Damian Lewis way.

When they read about the new camping in *Country Living* and *Country Life* (artless paeans sprinkled with stars slumming luxuriously in Rajasthani shikars with king-size beds and duck-down duvets), rain was not mentioned. Nor the unalloyed misery of frying eggs during a downpour, an experience that, despite portable Weber barbecues, has lost none of its let's-go-home imperative.

When Ceals and Francie were little and camped at the bottom of Francie's parents' garden, there was always an Aga to run back to; now they are imprisoned at a social frontier of righteous environmentalism. This was to be their escape after the school holidays, a green dream of respite from piano practice and homework, healthy living with stout walks and good books. They bought the nearest thing to a Kyrgyz domed yurt that Millets could provide, but it lacks the hand-stitched Mongolian embroidery element.

Celia says that given the campsite is not the Arcadian idyll of birdsong and noble oaks they'd envisaged, but on the edge of a perfectly hideous housing estate, it's lucky they didn't buy the Ted Baker tent adorned with flying ducks mounted on rose wallpaper plus a stag's head against a 1970s bamboo print. 'Competitive retro might have seriously upset our gingery friend.' They've been careful to conceal their Kidston sleeping bags, windbreaks and ponchos, while ostentatiously displaying tins of tomatoes implying they're regular spag bol types. Honestly, this was supposed to be cheaper than renting a cottage, but buying the cool kit has been exorbitant.

*Where is Sienna Miller in leopardette wellies
when you need her?*

Why eez it that the English drink so much?

The Italian in London

CARLA LIVES IN a state of permanent bemusement in Kensington. Why eez it that the Engleesh drink so much? Invite them to dinner and they treat her chardonnay, grapes picked by gnarled retainers on her ancestral estate in Alto Adige, like water. She bitterly resents giving them any Super Tuscan, grown and blended on her estate, Tenuta San Michele (acquired by a Medici uncle who was pope) near Florence. They just say it's jolly tolerable for a Chianti.

They eat in restaurants: 'We've a little trat round the corner, why don't you and Guido join us for a pasta fix?' Carla eats at home because she regards food in England as *merdoso*. Disgusting.

To protect herself from contamination she imports her own olive oil, harvested on the other family estates in Tuscany given to them by Grand Duke Cosimo I in 1500. So virgin it has never even seen a man, she sells it in the Conran Shop.

On frequent trips to Italy to oversee the children's schooling, she returns with prosciutto ham (from her own pigs), mushrooms and pasta. De Cecco is only a last resort. In summer, when she goes to Capri, Carla returns with tomatoes and lemons from Guido's family estate near Naples because as everyone knows, except the stupid Engleesh, the lemons and tomatoes from Naples are the best in the world.

Her Italian friends in London, who are nearly all related through energetic intermarriage, appreciate Carla's intolerance of anything save perfection. There is formality, even at lunch (linen napkins), and always three courses and gorgonzola oozing ripely.

A few amusing, if badly dressed (*tragico*, considering Savile Row tailoring) Engleesh intellectuals are allowed to cling to her table, even invited to her holiday house in Porto Ercoli. At Christmas she takes fearsome sums of money off them playing Mercante in Fiera.

The Party Animal

NARCISSI IS FURIOUS. What sort of party bag is this? Where is the MP3 player? Where is the Molly Brown jellybean necklace, enamel jellybeans in every colour (£30 each) on a silver chain (£12.50)? Where is the foot-long wand full of rainbow-coloured fairy dust that she can sprinkle down her nanny's bed? Narcissi is as fastidious about party bags as any Oscar nominee. Narcissi doesn't do homemade party bags with teddy purses, Narcissi likes Starbags, so Gwyneth, so Sadie, with tinted glasses and glow-in-the-dark 3D stickers. Narcissi wants lip gloss flavoured with starfruit, and a little bling tiara with Swarovski crystals and fluffy pink feathers.

No matter that Delphi's parents have taken over the whole of Hamley's for Delphi's fifth birthday: where is Narcissi's payola for wearing pink bows? She never liked Delphi anyway. Delphi's party was booorring compared to Iolanthe's in the zoo where they got to stroke snakes and everyone was given a hamster in a cage with a little locket on the door saying I ♥ Iolanthe. Narcissi stressed Hammy to death in four days, squeezing him through her fat fingers like a tube of toothpaste. He was so booorring. Petal's party was at the Natural History Museum and the sushi was from Nobu and Narcissi had to be restrained from climbing the dinosaur. That was booorring. Where was the dino-egg in the party bag? And at Cyclamen's party at the London Aquarium, where was the shark?

Narcissi cannot be fobbed off any more with sugar mice from Fortnum's. She knows her Armani from Accessorize in beaded purse-dom. Lollipops are so not cool unless in silver and shaped like an iPod. Novelty hairclips? Doesn't this mummy have a life? There was some ignorant mother who dared to put a book in Narcissi's party bag. Narcissi, as an act of defiance, stuck a party sparkly pencil in her ear and had to be taken to A&E.

Narcissi is as fastidious about party bags
as any Oscar nominee

The Savage Hangover

ARCHIE'S MOUTH FEELS like a rattlesnake's pit, with the rattlesnake still writhing in it. What a mistake to have that third bottle of Pomerol with Chalky White. And then the port, which seemed such a good idea at the time, when he was setting the world to rights in front of the dying embers of the fire and playing Wagner very loudly. The Valkyrie are now riding through his head.

He's tried Perrier but the bubbles were too cacophonous. There's nothing for it but two Nurofen Plus and the hair of the dog; thus Archie is racing to embrace his friend the voddy, crashing around the larder to find tomato juice, lemon, Worcestershire sauce and Tabasco, a treasure hunt punctuated by wails of distress at their absence.

Mrs Archie, in a vile humour from having been kept awake by the Wagner, has to be summoned to point out that all said ingredients are in front of his nose, bloody fool. She then evilly fries a lot of bacon, the smell of which contributes to Archie's tidal waves of nausea. He is not a well man. His hands are trembling like humming birds. He is never going to drink again, at least not before lunch on Christmas Day, for which he has some exceptional Meursault and a magnum of Léoville Barton. Until then, the old liver has run up a white flag.

That's after he's had the second Bloody Mary (because it isn't alcohol, in the circumstances it is a life support system). Woe that he had ever woken up – the world of the living is horribly bright, the sun having the temerity to shine, pulverising Archie's eyeballs. Dinner parties and Christmas parties are the invention of the devil for those with a delicate constitution.

Mrs Archie goes for the jugular with suggestions to chop logs and walk the dog, which is barking at ruinous decibels. Archie retreats, moaning piteously, to the lavatory.